HOW TO TEACH CHILDREN RESPONSIBILITY
EN71040

by
Harris Clemes, Ph.D.
Reynold Bean, Ed.M.

Edited by
Janet Gluckman

ENRICH
INSTRUCTIONAL
MATERIALS
DIVISION OF **OHAUS®** *presents* **THE WHOLE CHILD SERIES**

1980 Revised edition - Fifth Printing 1983
Copyright © 1978 Reynold Bean, Harris Clemes
Published by ENRICH, DIV./OHAUS, San Jose, CA 95131
All Rights Reserved Under International Convention
Printed in U.S.A.
ISBN 0-933358-78-4

CONTENTS

INTRODUCTION

Teaching them to be responsible is the single most important gift we can give our children.* Out of it will arise their ability to take care of themselves and to function as responsible adults in the real world.

We can build this virtue into our children by using their own experiences to show them the positive results of certain behaviors.

Children are flexible. They have to be, to put up with the things that we, as parents and teachers, do to them with the best of intentions. The problem is that we have to wait so many years before we can evaluate the product of our efforts. We need to have faith in our children and ourselves, and it helps if we use methods that have proven to be effective.

Fortunately, most children do grow up to be decent, mature, responsible adults. It is the waiting period that is so tough, the passage between childhood and maturity.

This handbook eases that process by providing tested methods that will help parents and teachers pass on to their children a high sense of self-esteem, good character, and an adequate set of goals and values—all of which are possible when children have the ability to be responsible.

The authors of this handbook have over thirty years of accumulated experience as family counselors, teachers and parents. We are convinced that teaching children to be responsible results in teaching them how to control their own lives in positive ways.

— The Authors

---

*He, rather than he or she, is used in the text for the sake of fluidity.

I.
What Is Responsibility?

According to the media, children are changing, and for the worse. We hear stories about extreme behavior in children; discussions of low scores on college qualifying exams, arguments about students' incompetence in basic skills, statistics showing delinquency on the rise, lurid stories of the children's pornography industry. We confront a steady flow of articles in national magazines regarding the trials and tribulations of children, and as a result, the trials and tribulations of parents.

With so many dramatic changes occurring in the world, it is reasonable to believe things are changing for children and adolescents too. Young people are not immune to the effect of larger social forces, and may well be barometers of change.

Surely children's behavior is affected by the press of social change, but many of their problems are stimulated by day-to-day experience, and are rooted in their early experiences within a family.

Making decisions about children is more difficult in a changing world. Parents who thought they were prepared for parenthood are confused about what it is they should be doing with, for, and to their children.

In this handbook, we do not blame parents, or any social institution for the difficulties that children are experiencing. Children are ultimately responsible for making choices and decisions about their own behavior, as any teacher, counselor, probation officer or policeman can attest. Many parents, striving their utmost to be adequate and responsible, find that their children continue to make decisions that make it difficult for them to cope with an increasingly complex world.

Though the title of this handbook is *How to Teach Children Responsibility,* we don't want to create the impression that we are going *back* to old verities about parenting: "Spare the rod and spoil the child," and "Good children are seen but not heard," don't help much when we face challenges to our own values. We need to look at those procedures that *can* go on within the family and are effective in giving children tools, attitudes and values to help them make decisions leading to productive and satisfying lives in a complex world.

Teaching children to be responsible requires a special *climate* within the home and school. Such a climate offers information about choices and consequences, and provides resources for making good choices.

What is responsibility? As the word implies, responsibility is the *ability to respond.* Through common usage, the word also implies making decisions that are appropriate and effective.

Appropriate means that a child makes most choices within the boundaries of social norms and expectations commonly held, to produce positive human relations, and to promote his own safety, success and security.

For example, if a child were to spit on the foot of a stranger who greeted him, it could be considered an inappropriate response. It would be so not because there is some absolute rule that a child does not spit on a stranger's foot, but because the relationship between the child and that person would likely become a negative one. On the other hand, if a child who is greeted by a stranger responds with a smile and says, "Hello. How are you?" it is likely that they will develop a positive relationship.

We needn't become too theoretical about what is appropriate. Even though people of good will may not reach the same conclusions about what is appropriate in every instance, the overwhelming number of relationships a child has are influenced by social norms, grace, tact and manners. Success and satisfaction in social interactions are a measure of a child's appropriateness, and such successes will reinforce his inclination to continue to act appropriately.

For a response to be *effective,* it must enable the child to accomplish goals that result in enhancing his own feelings of self-esteem. As an example, when a child wishes to visit a friend, he must secure permission from his parents to do so. If he asks without argument and in a straightforward manner, he is more likely to receive a positive response. *Even* parents, when treated with tact by a child, will respond amicably to a child's wishes.

In order for a child to respond effectively he needs to identify the features of a situation that are important. If he only exercises his own self-interest, and will not evaluate other's limits, he can create difficulties for himself *and* for others. For example, when parents need to meet a schedule that involves the whole family, they need to know that the children in the family will be ready on time and that no *one* member of the family will interfere with the rights of other members. Making choices that support the needs and interests of *others* is an important part of a child's sense of responsibility.

A child has to be aware of how others see things so that the choices he makes are influenced by the needs, rights, and responsibilities of others. As a child receives feedback from others, especially parents, he can refine his understanding of the way other people think about things. This increases the child's ability to be flexible, and makes him aware that standards and expectations may vary in different situations.

Children also need to be aware of their own needs and goals. A child is responsible when his actions creatively take into account his own goals *and* others' needs. Parents can help a child to arrive at this balance by helping him think through his own values and solve problems taking into account his own feelings. (See page 62.)

A child who has a sense of responsibility will increasingly experience success, and the rewards that result from success. A child who acts irresponsibly will experience more punishment and criticism than is his due, and self-esteem will diminish. He will not only *mistrust* his *own* reactions, and the way others react to him; he will also develop a negative attitude toward life.

In order to teach children to be responsible, there must be some "quid-pro-quo." It is difficult for a child to increase his ability to be responsible if he doesn't get rewards *and* praise for such behavior. On the other hand, a child will continue to be irresponsible if he receives excessive criticism, ridicule or shame.

One of the difficulties that children have in learning responsibility is the requirement that sometimes personal gratification must be deferred until agreements with others have been fulfilled. There is often no *immediate* reward for acting appropriately, and sometimes just what a child will receive for doing or acting well may be unclear. If a child can depend on parental consistency in providing periodic rewards for responsible behavior, it eases the problem of deferred gratification. Children may have to be reminded that there will be a "pay-off"—and parents must be sure to fulfill any promises made. Children who are rewarded for being responsible will gradually develop an awareness that responsibility and good feelings are associated. In time, their need for external rewards will diminish.

Being responsible means that a child will have to make some decisions that produce discomfort. A child who is required to perform duties may often

7

have to do them instead of some other activity that is more fun or satisfying. The ability to perform tasks *in spite* of discomfort is necessary in order to be responsible. Helping children deal with this issue is a major task. Parents need to remind children that such discomforts are usually temporary, and result in the *greater* comforts from praise, affection, or rewards received for doing jobs well. Young children need their parents to be patient and tolerant of their dilemma, since they usually cannot verbalize it clearly.

Many children experience difficulties in situations where being responsible means balancing obligations to others against their own impulses. Children are prone to act impulsively and often don't evaluate situations according to what consequences may occur. Parents must teach children how to make choices that may conflict with the impulse to play or have a good time. Paradoxically, a good deal of impulsive behavior in young children results from feelings of *safety and security*. Feeling safe gives a child the privilege of expressing feelings without excessive concern for painful consequences.

This handbook presumes that children *are* responsible for broad areas of their life, and *always* need to be held responsible for what they do and say. It's true that children will make errors in judgment, when they lack experience and information. Parents need to be tolerant and patient as a child gains experience and information. Nevertheless it is the parents who must assess the level of responsibility that children are capable of meeting, and build rules and standards in the family to support and encourage responsible behavior. *If children are not held accountable for their actions, it will be more difficult for them to learn from their experiences.*

Teaching children to be *responsible* is not the same as teaching children to be *guilty.* Children who have a sense of responsibility have the tools, attitudes and resources they need to evaluate situations effectively and make choices that are appropriate to themselves and those around them. Children who are motivated by guilt, *seeming* to be responsible, have "special" criteria for making choices. They wish to avoid punishment or pain; they can't tolerate disagreement, or criticism; and they have an excessive need to gain approval from adults. The differences between guilty children and responsible ones are seen in the following table:

	Children who are motivated by guilt.	Children who have a sense of responsibility.
Goals of Their Behavior	To *avoid* pain, punishment, criticism, or disapproval.	To *satisfy* needs of themselves or others.
Methods They Use	Placating, dependent on others, rigid in their approach to new situations.	Independence, flexibility, being forthright.
Focus of Their Attention	In the past, on memories of pain or criticism, old situations that are safe.	In the present or future— experiencing pleasure now, or seeking new goals. Remembering successful experiences of the past.
Feelings about Themselves	Self-recriminating, anxious and fearful, low self-esteem.	Self-approving and positive, high self-esteem.

In this handbook, we will show you how to teach children to be responsible in a way that diminishes a child's guilt and self-condemnation. The methods described will increase a child's ability to make choices and decisions that lead to a greater sense of self-worth. This, after all, is the reason for being responsible.[1]

II.
The Evolution of Responsibility in a Child

Responsibility is not genetic. It has to be learned through experience. An infant begins life with few resources for self-maintenance and no responsibility for the safety or happiness of himself or others. By adulthood, he must be able to take responsibility for everything that happens in his life. From the first day of life until adulthood, a child must advance his capability to take responsibility. He acquires an understanding for the importance of being responsible through everyday interactions with his parents, his teachers, and his peers.

These interactions involve expectations that are held for him and which he must learn to respond to with increasing appropriateness and effectiveness. Early in a child's life such expectations need to be communicated as clearly as possible, relative to his ability to understand. As a child responds to these expectations, he needs to receive feedback about how well he is meeting them, and simultaneously, be shown alternatives that increase his ability to deal with a variety of situations.

A sense of responsibility arises from:

- Being given responsibility.

- Receiving feedback about the effectiveness of one's responses.

- Having information about alternatives that are appropriate in a variety of situations.

11

The number of situations that a child will take responsibility for will increase as he matures. The things he takes responsibility for will change, and his ability to *be* responsible will become more refined. As an example: it is not unusual for a two or three year old to respond to people by crying, withdrawing, or hiding behind his mother's skirts. Such a reaction would, however, be highly inappropriate in a fourteen or fifteen year old. If a child is exposed to a broad array of experiences, and learns to deal with a variety of expectations, his "catalog" of effective responses will grow.

We learn, in great measure, from the mistakes we make. But if a child cannot learn *why* something was a mistake, or *what* his alternatives were— he cannot improve. We often meet people who make the same mistake over and over again, because they don't know any better alternatives.

Children are always learning to balance self-interest against responsibility to others. Understanding how we are responsible to and for others grows as we mature.

Children are usually motivated by self-interest. This is neither a sign of their decadence nor sinfulness, but rather an appropriate early stage in learning to be responsible for and to *themselves. Self-interest and being responsible to oneself are not the same.* The former is characterized by denial or disregard for the needs of others; the latter by considering the effect of others on ourselves and vice versa. With maturity comes the recognition that fulfilling responsibilities to others *is* in our own self-interest.

Helping children evolve a sense of responsibility through childhood and adolescence requires that parents be patient and tolerant, while remaining clear and consistent about what they expect.

If parents and teachers recognize that children *will* make mistakes, but need to be told about their mistakes *and* the alternatives available to them, a firm sense of responsibility that will carry into adulthood can be ensured.

III.
The Importance of Decision-Making

Being responsible does not mean following orders in a "lock-step" manner. If all important decisions about what he is to do are being made by others, a child is just being the "agent" for carrying out the will of adults. Being responsible means making choices and decisions for oneself that result in positive outcomes. If children don't have the opportunity to make important decisions, they cannot act responsibly. Children's capability to make effective decisions varies from time to time, and from child to child, and there are some decisions that children should not make because of their age, maturity, and experience. In order to teach children to be responsible, opportunities for making decisions need to be maximized and expanded as early as possible.

A climate in which children are expected to make decisions must be created within the home and classroom. Decision-making needs to become a *conscious process* for children. They must be made aware that they are making decisions and are expected to make them.

Decision-making is essentially the same as problem-solving. When we are confronted with a problem, we analyze and evaluate it in order to make a decision about what to do. *Children who learn to make decisions effectively are better problem-solvers.* Parents and teachers have to help children understand that there are *alternatives* available in most situations and the decision they make is a selection of one of them.

Children make many decisions every day. One of the criteria of growth is to become aware of these decisions and the way they are made. Parents and teachers help children develop their decision-making skills by pointing out to them the ways in which they do make decisions, and the results that occur from making good decisions. These are decisions that meet the child's needs as well as the needs of others.

Being able to make decisions *well* is the chief factor in developing a sense of power or control over the circumstances of one's life. Having such a sense of control or influence is necessary in order to have high self-esteem and a firm sense of self-worth. (See page 62.)

Indecisiveness = Irresponsibility

Because of the relationship between decision-making and responsibility, it is apparent that being *indecisive* is a way of being *irresponsible*. Being indecisive when a choice is required makes it necessary for other people to take responsibility for making choices. When children are indecisive, they will often manipulate parents and teachers into making decisions for them. This is neither unusual nor inappropriate in young children, who may lack information and experience. They may be cautious in the face of negative consequences that might occur if they make a poor decision. A pattern of indecisiveness is indicative that a child is not developing a sense of responsibility.

Sometimes children get bored at home, and can't seem to find anything to do. So they come to a parent or teacher and ask: "What can I do?" Suggestions may be rejected with negative expressions, like "That's no fun!" or the child may try it for awhile, get bored again, and come back for another suggestion. After some time, most parents will be driven to distraction and begin to get angry. In spite of the fact that a child who is caught up in this pattern may know just about everything there is to do at home, he nevertheless wants someone else to make decisions, and share in the blame for his bored feelings. Parents dislike punishing a child for not having something to do, but it's hard to avoid if this kind of pattern repeats itself.

Teachers see the same pattern at work. If a child avoids making decisions to do school work, teachers must make extraordinary efforts to encourage the child to perform a task at a satisfactory level. When a child continues to avoid effort, the teacher is usually held accountable for not providing adequate resources or methods. What is overlooked, though, is that the child's indecisiveness (irresponsibility) is often the central issue.

One of the problems teachers have to deal with is children who repeatedly come to them with questions they already have the answers to. Such children will ask so many questions (one teacher timed such a child over a period of days and found that he averaged one question per minute) that they effectively maneuver the teacher into doing the work for them. If a teacher finally becomes impatient with this behavior, the child may cease doing any work.

Being decisive always involves taking risks. Children are often faced with making decisions when adequate information is lacking. Decisiveness often means making a commitment to a course of action where the consequences are not clear. As we have pointed out previously, there is a clear relationship between a child's ability to make decisions and high self-esteem. Children with high self-esteem are able to take risks with greater confidence. When children's self-esteem is low, parents and teachers must reduce the level of risk, so they can make decisions with greater security. Some examples of low and high risk decisions are:

Lower Risk	Higher Risk
1. Would you like to do A or B?	1. What would you like to do?
2. Do three of these problems.	2. Do as many problems as you can.
3. Please sit here.	3. Where would you like to sit?
4. When you finish two problems, let me check them.	4. If you have any questions, ask me to help.

Lowering risks means reducing ambiguity about a problem or task. Making communication as clear and specific as possible helps children to make decisions with confidence.

To help a child act decisively, parents and teachers must provide the resources that allow him to make decisions with a high degree of security. Parents who encourage children to make decisions in spite of their indecisiveness or apprehension, are helping them to become more responsible to themselves and to others.

Having a Sense of Limits

Children who do not have such a sense of limits often make choices that result in problems for themselves, and impose discomforts on others. When children do have a *sense of limits* they recognize that some choices may place them outside the bounds of appropriate or effective behavior, and may result in excessive pain or punishment. Such children "check" their alternatives before jumping into situations or making important decisions.

A child develops a "sense of limits" by living within limits, and recognizing that they are always present. Having a sense of limits is like having a built-in warning system; a child realizes before making a decision that it may have unacceptable consequences.

Parents and teachers can help establish a sense of limits by creating a system where limits are apparent and clear, and where consequences for exceeding them are predictable and consistent. This helps a child to refine the quality of his decisions. Without such a sense, the alternatives are often too broad for a child to make good choices.

A sense of limits developed early in a child's life may bring out some fear and apprehension. It is appropriate for a child to have some fear about limits, but this will dissipate over time, as the child recognizes that limits and their consequences are consistent. Fear disappears when a child becomes aware of the alternatives in a situation, and can make good predictions about the consequences of choosing one of those alternatives.

Parents and teachers can help build a sense of limits through a number of practices:

- They need to clarify *for themselves* what they expect children to do or not do.

- Expectations, including responsibility for chores and duties, need to be stated in ways children can understand.

- They should find out if a child understands expectations by having him repeat them, or by guiding the child through them.

- Time limits for doing chores and/or simple schoolwork must be clear, unambiguous and reasonable.

- Consequences for non-performance must be stated to the child. Those consequences must be applied consistently without undue guilt or remorse, *and* without excessive pain to the child. Consistency is more important than severity.

- All rules and duties should be written and posted, so that "forgetting" cannot be an excuse.

- Both parents (if available) need to participate in explaining rules to children. Then they know that *both* parents will uphold them.

- All children in the family or classroom should have comparable responsibilities, with appropriate adjustments for age and capabilities.[2]

IV.
When Duties Are No Longer Fun for Children

It is never too early to teach children to be responsible. Even during infancy parents can imply limits and encourage decision making. For example, a mother who attempts to mollify her crying child when diapers are being changed is beginning to instruct about attitudes she wants the child to have under such circumstances. Parents start to help a child make decisions by providing a rattle the child seems to want, or responding to wishes he expresses.

Even though these simple activities are the foundations of responsibility, we don't presume that a child will begin to work as soon as he begins to walk. Early in a child's life, taking responsibility is usually associated with play.

Playing is an important factor in preparing a child to be responsible. The following definitions of work and play might help parents foresee some of the dilemmas both parents and children may experience:

"Play" defines those activities children do *because of the way they feel. Play is a response to wishes, desires and wants.*

"Work" covers those activities children do *in spite of the way* they feel. It involves deferring gratification, putting off things they want to do in order to fulfill obligations to others.

Parents, and later teachers, need to provide a balance between work and play as children grow. Even though play can teach children processes and skills, they also need to be required to perform tasks that are not play.

Children will find "work" to be "playful" if activities are associatd with good feelings and warmth and humor. Asking a child to pick up a *few* toys while Momma is cleaning up the house can make him feel like a "big helper." When a child takes a few items out to the garbage with Daddy, he is doing a "grown-up" chore. Putting blocks away in a box in time to music makes cleaning up a game. Allowing a toddler to switch the vacuum cleaner on and off while Mother cleans is often a "big thrill" to him. Similarly, in the classroom, what is usually seen as work can be turned into "play" and vice-versa.

After a time of playing "cleaning up," "putting away toys," etc., the "game" wears off. What had been play has turned into work and is no longer "fun." An important parenting/teaching skill is to know how to make the transition from play to work, so that children comfortably evolve a sense of responsibility to themselves, their own belongings, and the people around them.

Children mimic attitudes about work and play from the adults they model—usually their parents and teachers. If parents find work onerous and avoid it, children will mimic that attitude. All young children wish to be like their parents. If a child sees one or both parents avoiding responsibilities, he will usually develop a similar attitude. If Daddy never does the dishes, a boy child may feel it is "unmanly" to do so. If parents or older siblings use profanity, a small child will repeat the "best" words. If Momma gets angry when cleaning, a toddler will associate negative feelings with these duties. If parents and teachers approach their own tasks with good will, patience, and a firm sense of responsibility, they will create a climate where the child's efforts at learning to work will be associated with positive feelings.

In making the transitions from play to work, clear standards and expectations are required. A child may progress from putting away toys as a game, to putting them away in order to help Mommy or teacher, to doing so because the adult can't do it right now, to putting away toys because they're his responsibility.

Each of these transition points involves some stress and confusion. If the adults are patient through such changes, and continue to require the child to perform in certain ways that are rewarded, these transitions can be made painlessly, and the child will assume responsibilities with the least possible resistance.

Children will learn to take responsibility if:

- Children know how to make decisions, and their good decisions have been noted and reinforced with appropriate rewards.

- Parents and teachers are aware of the decisions a child makes, and ensure that opportunities to make decisions are available. Adults should create a climate that emphasizes individual responsibility and diminishes blaming, indecisiveness and irresponsibility.

- Parents and teachers avoid making decisions that children are capable of making. Making decisions for children undermines the ability to be irresponsible.

Children profit, especially during toddlerhood, from being able to make decisions that influence their parents' behavior. As an example, if a father has made a decision to play with his child for a given period of time, he can say: "Let's play in your room and not make too much noise. What would you like to do?" or children can make decisions about things like:

- what to play with in the bath
- the clothes they want to wear
- what they want for snacks
- what book they wish to have read to them

Children do not need to be in control all the time (and shouldn't be), but if they know that the parent will allow them control of some interactions, their sense of self-worth and competence will grow, and will assist them to develop a sense of responsibility.

V.
Blocks to Teaching Children Responsibility

There are many factors that influence how children assume responsibility, and whether parents and teachers will effectively teach it. Knowing what interferes with effectively teaching children responsibility will help you gain perspective on your relationship to your children, understand your own blocks to being an effective teacher, and prepare you to deal with your own and your child's feelings in a positive manner.

Parents' Guilt and Its Consequences

Being a parent is one of the most ordinary things in the world. Most members of the human race have performed the role. But in spite of the fact that billions of people have been parents, being one remains a difficult task. Each new generation must face the paradoxes and ambiguities of this responsibility.

The chief block to being an effective parent is the experience of guilt.

Guilt results when we believe that what we're doing, and how we're doing it, does not measure up to our expectations of ourselves. If the distance between our expectations of ourselves and our performance as we judge it is great, we will experience more guilt. In order to reduce guilt, we have to lower our expectations to a reasonable level, improve our performance, or do both simultaneously.

All parents receive messages from preceding generations and their own peers about how they "should" be as parents. These "shoulds" influence behavior enormously. The inordinate amount of advice for parents appearing in every medium—books, television, radio—ensures that many parents will have expectations they are not living up to.

All parents experience guilt when they believe they are causing pain or discomfort to their children. When you interfere with something your children wish to do, or insist that they do something they don't wish to do, they complain. Crying, pouting, and making accusations about parents' motives or character are techniques children use to resist fulfilling duties or responsibilities parents may insist upon.

Parents react to these signs of pain or discomfort by pausing to re-evaluate how they are handling a situation. They try to find some new path which will assuage children's feelings, and re-establish warmth and affection between themselves and their children.

Guilt is a decidedly uncomfortable feeling. Because of this, parents have many ways to mask their own guilt from themselves, and not identify it. People mask their guilt feelings by:

- translating guilt into anger, and displacing it on someone else. Parents often displace it on each other: "If it weren't for what you do, our child would act properly (the way I want him to)!"

- blaming things on circumstances that are beyond one's control: "He's just like Uncle Joe; there's nothing I can do about it."

- developing body ailments that excuse one from taking action: "Every time I argue with her, I get a headache; I learned to avoid her."

- taking all the responsibility, rather than dealing with conflict: "When I ask him to do something, he puts up such a fuss that it's easier to do it myself."

- making up elaborate or unreasonable rationalizations for avoiding situations that produce guilt feelings: "I feel it's very important that she knows that I love her, and it's liable to shake her confidence if I get angry."

Guilt makes parents change the ways they deal with children. All of you have heard of the importance of being *consistent* with children. When parents do something that causes pain or discomfort to children, and experience guilt or remorse, they tend to alter what they set out to do, relax limits, or not follow through with threats. When parents don't do what they said they would, it automatically results in inconsistency, and the child knows it.

Parents who are subject to excessive guilt create insecurity in their children. When children sense that parents lack confidence in what they're doing, they become aware of their parents' confusion about authority and control. Young children feel more secure if they have a consistent sense of parental authority and control, even though they try to influence parents' behavior. Parents who are inconsistent because of guilt will communicate, unwittingly, that they are not in control. When children sense that parents' authority is tentative or ambivalent, they become anxious. *Anxious children will misbehave more than children who are not anxious.* The connection between excessive parental guilt and children's misbehavior is shown over and over again; parents who feel most guilty have the most difficulty in managing their children.

When children are anxious because their parents are not in control, *they try to clarify standards of behavior and limits through manipulation and power plays.*

In every family there are several important functions that must be fulfilled. These functions are:

- providing *predictability* in the lives of family members so as to reduce anxiety, i.e. who will do what when, and in what manner?

- *coordinating* the activities of the family, so that everyone can get done what they need to do.

- *setting standards* so that each member of the family knows what's expected, and can depend on others to fulfill responsibilities while knowing how to fulfill their own.

- providing a climate for *good communication*, so that needs and wants can be voiced and heard, which increases the level of personal comfort of all family members.

If parents don't perform these functions, the children must, inevitably, try to. We can assume that children will have less skill and foresight in doing so. That leaves us with the fact that if parents neglect these functions, chaos is likely to result.

Why Parents Find It Hard to Punish

When parents try to teach responsibility, they need a method for holding children accountable for their behavior. In order for children to be accountable, parents must respond to rule infractions. These responses are consequences or punishments.

Parents who find it difficult to apply punishments have a hard time teaching their children to be responsible, because they lack "the clout"with which to hold their children accountable. Children need *some* pressure to encourage them to seek alternative ways to act that meet the standards of family and social life.

All parents want their children to be happy and satisfied, in addition to being well-behaved. It is a rare child who will appear to be happy and satisfied when faced with punishment. Children usually make some effort to "fight back," by showing negative feelings or taking parents to task for punishing them.

Many parents feel they have failed if they need to punish a child for misbehavior. Children are not born knowing how to behave. Much of what they learn occurs through trial and error. The errors need to be illuminated by consequences that occur. It is only fair that consequences be clarified ahead of time by parents. Consequences are not the same thing as threats. A consequence is a pre-determined course of action that both children and parents know is inevitable under specific circumstances. A threat is a message to a child that parents are becoming upset and are losing control. Threats are not usually carried out, creating a climate of inconsistency and anxiety.

Punishment of children is not a sign of parental failure. The ability to punish children for misbehavior is evidence that parents mean what they say and are willing to follow through. When children understand that parents mean what they say, are consistent in following through, and are *fair-minded and reasonable* when imposing punishments, they are less likely to misbehave. Children who know there will be consequences for misbehavior assess the likely consequences of various alternatives, before deciding how to act.

Some parents find it hard to punish because they view their children as part of themselves, and not as autonomous individuals. When punishing, they experience more pain than the child experiences. When parents don't treat them as separate individuals, it is difficult for children to develop their own individuality. Children whose uniqueness is not recognized will often seek recognition through misbehavior.

Sometimes parents believe it is necessary to be angry in order to punish. Anger is not necessary if consequences have been clarified for a specific rule infraction. Anger and resentment result when parents have no clear way to control children's behavior, or from using techniques that don't work. Parents need to control the way resentment confuses their relationship with children, and avoid excessive anger. But, a parent who can totally avoid resentment or anger is probably a saint. The ordinary parent is going to have to deal with these feelings many times. Having a clear set of guidelines for behavior, within and outside of the family, and clear consequences attached to not meeting these standards, minimizes the likelihood of anger and resentment. When limits are clear, children can explore alternatives within those limits, and make safe and appropriate choices.

Another reason many parents find it hard to punish is the fear of damaging their child's "psyche." Some children react so dramatically to the imposition of consequences that it appears as if they might be going "crazy." If a child can convince parents that punishments are affecting his emotional stability, then he ought to receive an award for good acting.

Children's psyches are "damaged" by living in families where emotional outbursts are excessive; where there's a high degree of inconsistency; where they cannot find out what standards apply in different situations; where parents are so ambivalent and anxiety-ridden that they create a "hyper-emotional" climate; and where parents punish misbehavior but do not reward the child's efforts to act appropriately. When parents teach children to be responsible, these things are avoided.

Parents' Childhood Influences Their Own Behavior

In spite of all the books, manuals, documentation on TV, and public discussion of child-rearing practices, most parents are influenced by their own background when deciding how to raise their own children.

We either *respond* to our childhoods by continuing the practices that we learned in our own families, or else we *react* in an opposite way, by trying to avoid being like our own parents.

Trying not to be like our parents is very difficult. It can make us feel uncomfortable, awkward, and mechanical. Many parents experienced difficulties as children, often because of parents who were insensitive or abusive. When we attempt to avoid perpetuating the worst excesses we experienced, we bend over backwards to avoid doing the same things, and often go to extremes.

Simple and reasonable answers to common problems become complicated when parents bring emotional overlays from their own childhood into relationships with their own children. When a parent interacts with his child, particularly under stress, he may momentarily forget himself, mimicking his own mother or father in a similar, but distant past, circumstance. ("Put on your sweater! I'm cold. *My* mother always made me wear one.") At every stage of our child's development, we can make new choices and decisions as to how we are going to handle situations. We can apply the best current thinking we have to the situation at hand.

The things we remember from our own childhoods are highly emotional experiences. We carry the experiences in our memories and are reminded of them when our children pass through the stages in which we experienced something significant. At such points, we tend to handle our children as we were handled at that time in our own lives. We will respond in the same way, again and again, even though we know that what we are doing is making our relationship with our own children irrational.

In order to reduce the negative effects of the past, parents only need to be willing to try some new alternatives. When we try something new, and are successful, our self-esteem rises, and we are automatically less bound to old, irrational patterns.

VI.
Resentment: How It Grows in Parents and Affects Children

Most parents show resentment towards their children only under special circumstances. These include: when they are talking to a counselor who is sympathetic and understanding; when they have had a few drinks that reduce inhibitions; or *when they blow up and get angry for an infraction which is very minor in itself.*

Resentment toward a child is a sign that there is an unresolved power struggle between parent and child, and that the parent feels he's losing. This feeling results from not performing some of the functions of responsible parenting, including being clear about expectations and consequences.

Grievances between parents and children are nearly impossible to avoid. Children often have reasonable grievances about the way they've been treated or about promises that have not been kept. We tend to forget that parents can have grievances against their children for things *they* said or did that offended the parent. Many parents find it hard to communicate these grievances. Grievances have a way of remaining unless there is some way to resolve them or communicate about them. Parents who are either unwilling or incapable of communicating their grievances to their children will inevitably build up resentment.

Here are some simple guidelines that can help parents communicate grievances to children:

- Describe what happens rather than blaming the child.

  "When you spend so much time on the phone, I can't use it or get calls."

  not

  "All you care about is yourself and your friends."

- Be specific about the behavior that bothers you, rather than putting labels on the child's character or personality.

  "When you come into the kitchen when I'm cooking, I get distracted and forget something important. Please stay out until I tell you it's OK."

  not

  "Are you blind or stupid? Can't you see I'm busy?"

- Own your own feelings rather than making the child responsible for them.

  "I get angry when you talk to me in that tone of voice."

  not

  "You make me angry when you argue."

- Invite the child to participate in solving the problem.

  "What do you think can be done to get your room cleaner?"

  not

  "If you can't get your room clean then you'll just be punished again and again."

Parents become frustrated when they are unable to influence their child's behavior. There are times when parents cannot make something happen unless the child agrees to participate. On many occasions children will resist parents even at the risk of being punished simply because they are not allowed to participate in the solution. Parents should encourage children to participate in problem solving, before getting into head-to-head struggles.

Sometimes parents' resentment is their own responsibility and not only the child's fault. There are times when parents want children to do something in a specific way, but have not clearly communicated what they expect. If parents have not taken the time to clarify what they want from their children, then poor performance is to be expected. Sometimes parents have higher expectations than their children can meet at that time.

Parents' expectations can be too high for a number of reasons:

- Asking the child to do something that he isn't capable of: *they're too little, not strong enough, lack experience, etc.*

- Not clarifying what you want and how it's to be done.

- Not providing the necessary resources for the child to perform the task well.

- Not demonstrating the process so that the child can *observe* what to do.

- Not checking whether the child understood in the first place.

It is to a child's advantage to have parents feel slightly resentful. No parent wants to feel resentful toward a child, and any parent who does is likely to feel guilty. When parents feel guilty about feeling resentful, they will often give in, and give the child what he wants.

In the struggle between the child's desire for freedom, autonomy, and self-interest, and the parents' need for authority and control, the child's ability to produce resentment is a powerful weapon. As long as parents tolerate a power struggle and play their part in keeping it going, resentment in parents and children is the inevitable consequence.

The feelings between parent and child are different if, instead of a power struggle, communication is open, clear and honest. The parents set the standard for communication in the family, and children will follow that model. Parents who make it a practice to be clear and direct with their children will find that their children will reciprocate.

"It's Easier to Do It Myself"

How often have you heard yourself saying those words, usually with a great deal of resentment, and how many more times have you thought them? Teaching children to be responsible is no easy task. On many occasions, it *is* easier for parents to "do it themselves." But, one of the paradoxes of being a parent is that we often have to forego efficiency in favor of teaching children to do things on their own. This paradox never ceases as long as our children remain with us.

Often the motive for the "do it myself" attitude is that parents want to avoid creating discomfort for a child, and hence, for themselves. Sometimes it seems that children are not able to learn some of the things that we want them to. They make strenuous efforts that seem to be fraught with pain and discomfort until we take onto *ourselves* the responsibility for performing a task.

The problem with the "it's easier to do it myself" approach is that whenever we take back a responsibility that we gave to a child, we also store up some resentment and frustration we will "pay back" to the child sooner or later. If parents want a child to do something, and become frustrated by his incompetent performance, they feel resentment, knowing their authority has been frustrated. This resentment will come out towards some member of the family. Taking back responsibilities rarely produces positive results in the long run.

Children lose out when parents feel "it's easier to do it myself." They lose an opportunity to learn something that will develop their own competence, and they are not being held accountable for some task they're expected to do.

Wanting to *avoid conflict* is an important motive for "doing it myself." Many parents avoid conflict with their children, and find it easier to take on more and more responsibilities. One parent may fear criticism and will take on additional responsibilities in order to placate the other parent, but the children are the losers.

Parents need to balance out their *teaching* vs. *nurturing* roles. The role of parent as nurturer is characterized by warmth, affection, love, sympathy, etc. The teaching role requires distance or dispassion. Teachers, to be effective, must be able to tolerate any discomfort they create in their students. It is important for parents, too, to stand back, evaluate their child's performance with objectivity, and make decisions that are reasonable in terms of the child's needs.

A Teacher	A Nurturer
• holds a child accountable for what he does	• tries to make a child comfortable
• wants a child to be able to act independently	• wants a child to know that he is loved and protected
• has standards by which the child's performance is judged	• provides rewards in order to make a child feel good
• emphasizes growth and challenge	• tries to fulfill a child's needs

- provides rewards in proportion to a child's performance

- tries to ensure that a child makes decisions

Children want parents to be "nurturers" so they will experience less pain or discomfort. A nurturer reduces discomfort for the one who is being nurtured. The best teachers recognize that discomfort is often the price paid for understanding and growth.

What Good Teachers Do

1. *Break down tasks* into small steps so that a child can perform each one well.

2. *Provide praise* or other rewards when a child successfully performs each step.

3. *Make clear* what standards are going to be used for evaluating performance.

4. *Provide evaluations* that include feedback about what was done correctly *and* incorrectly.

5. *Offer demonstrations* so that a child can *see* what he's to do.

6. *Work with* the child to solve any problems that arise in the course of doing a job.

VII.
How Children Respond When Others Wish Them to Be Responsible

Children are ambivalent about others' efforts to make them responsible. Being responsible means being held accountable, and that means they will often face limits to doing what they want. A child will be both positive and negative, hot and cold, toward wishes for them to be responsible. Parents and teachers need to be prepared for an on-again-off-again attitude by children about being responsible.

Children are often caught in a double-bind that everyone experiences. It has been labelled the *self/other dilemma*.

Everyone has to balance a desire to please *self* against the obligation to meet the needs of *others*. In children, this most often shows up as a conflict between wanting to please themselves and wanting to please parents. The wise parent recognizes that *both* motives are in a child, often simultaneously. The child is asking: "What's in this for me, and what's in it for you?"

If children don't experience rewards for taking responsibility, they will reach the conclusion that there's not much in it for them.

Children will be responsible if they find that it results in some advantage to them. Since parents control the resources for rewards, they must be willing to use them in a way that convinces the child that there is an advantage to being responsible.

39

These resources include parents' time, interest, support, and good will. Children feel that there is little advantage to obeying parents or being responsible if they cannot earn these rewards.

Rewarding children for good behavior is important, and parents need to be aware of the various kinds of rewards that they can give. Many parents believe that "rewards" for good behavior are a form of "bribery." Rewards of a material kind (money, toys, etc.), may become bribes if they are the chief technique that parents use to motivate children, and if children learn that by holding out long enough, they get something for acting appropriately. Rewards are those things that a child values—things he wants or needs. We want to emphasize *non-material* rewards as alternatives:

- **Give children verbal recognition and praise** for jobs that are well done: "You did a fantastic job in cleaning out your closet."

- **Provide spontaneous recognition,** periodically, that is connected to children's accomplishments: "How would you like to go and get an ice cream cone; you really worked hard cleaning the bathroom."

- **Give children support** when they need it: "Since you helped me weed the garden yesterday, it seems as if I can help you with your homework tonight."

- **Show interest** in what children do, and encourage them: "Since you have to go to a scout meeting tonight, I'll do the dishes for you."

- **Share chores** with children from time to time as recognition of their efforts: "You've really been doing a good job on your room; how would you like some help today?"

Why Children Don't Feel Bad If They Are Irresponsible

"Feeling bad" for acting irresponsibly results from a mature moral and ethical attitude. Moral values are learned through experience, from modeling others, and from instruction. Adults will be sadly disappointed if they assume that young children are so sensitive to the moral implications of their behavior that feelings of guilt or remorse will promote self-control. Children often don't understand the moral issues that apply in their relationships with parents and teachers, and may not understand when they are being offensive.

Self-interest is a dominant motive in childhood. In fact, it's a dominant motive throughout life, except that mature adults have found many ways to exercise *their* self-interest without interfering with the needs of *others*.

Feelings of remorse or guilt interfere with actions that express self-interest. When children are remorseful or guilty, their only way to alleviate the feeling is to be more dutiful to what parents or other authority figures want them to do. Those feelings, then, result in children acquiescing to rules laid down by others, in an obsessive way.

Adults often try to qualify the natural self-interest of children by having them "feel bad" through guilt. Ethical behavior, though, does not evolve from guilt, but from a child becoming aware of how to balance self-interest and the rights of others. An ethical sense is only gained through experience, and children need time to develop it. Guilt and remorse often stop the development of such an awareness, diminishing a child's self-esteem and promoting a need to placate others.

When adults want children to feel remorseful or guilty, they attempt to stimulate these feelings with questions such as, "Don't you feel bad for having done that to your sister?" or "How would you like it if someone did that to you?" or "If you grow up with attitudes like that you'll have a hard time." That may be expecting children to feel things that they are not capable of feeling.

Parents and teachers believe, and rightfully so, that if they can change a child's attitude, they will have greater control over the child's behavior. But, changing a child's attitude is more difficult than influencing behavior directly. Much frustration and resentment surround this issue. It is important to keep your eye on children's behavior when they are young and developing, not on trying to change their attitudes. Neither parents nor teachers can change attitudes until a child has collected a great deal of experience, both within the home and outside of it, that "proves" to the child, through his own experience, that an attitude or belief needs to change. When a child has an "attitude" that adults want to change they can best do so by clarifying their expectations and requiring more appropriate behavior. While it may be hard to *change* an attitude, parents may *influence* it by *their own behavior*. Children may not change an attitude quickly, but they do *observe* what others do and say, and gradually integrate this information into their own ideas of what is right to do.

Expectations need to be communicated clearly and simply, so children can learn what they need to do. When parents' expectations and children's expectations are the same, for example, there is no conflict. When children understand some of the simple ways they can please parents, at no cost to themselves, they often will adopt those behaviors to increase the likelihood that they will receive rewards and praise. If a child can please parents only at some cost to himself, resentment and frustration will grow. And as they do grow, the likelihood of misbehavior will also grow.

The basic strategy that is needed is to help children learn how to meet expectations at the same time that they find some satisfaction for themselves. This requires the liberal use of the rewards that are at your command.

How Children Sabotage Adult Decisions

Children have a number of strategies to undermine adults' purposes. In response, those adults experience frustration and powerlessness in trying to control or manage children.

Children's attempts to avoid responsibility often border on being reasonable. A parent or teacher may feel that child is purposefully making efforts to avoid things, but his "sabotage" tactics may be so subtle that there is little to challenge him about because of the "apparent" reasonableness of the strategy.

Children sabotage parents' efforts by developing the reputation of being incompetent or irresponsible. If a child consistently does chores in a manner that is incompetent, adults may conclude that he's incapable of learning, and back off from requiring him to perform certain duties. Any child who is "fortunate" enough to have such a reputation will find himself not being asked to do things, and may be comfortable being the family or classroom "idiot."

Foot dragging is used to avoid completion of tasks. When using this strategy, children do things so slowly, or need so many reminders that parents throw up their hands and say: "It's easier to do it myself."

Some children "never quite don't" do something. They also never quite do it. They appear to make valiant efforts; they make several false starts. Early in the process of doing something they voice their confusion, frustration, or pain. Children who employ this strategy can rarely be punished for not doing something, because they can say: "Look how hard I tried."

There are children who do things incompletely. They make a great public display of trying to be accommodating, but when they "finish" the task, parents observe that it has not been done completely. It is difficult, at that point, to berate the child with the fact that something *hasn't* been done, because so much of it *has* been done. If this strategy is employed regularly by the child, parents and teachers soon come to *expect* that the job will not be completely done, and will give it to someone else or complete it themselves.

Nit-pickers are children who enjoy arguing about tasks, and will invariably find some minor point to haggle about. Even though parents are reasonable in what they ask, nit-pickers will find something unclear or "unfair." These children enjoy *talking* about tasks, rather than doing them, and will, if allowed to, talk them to death.

"Jail house lawyers" will follow the "letter of the law" to extremes, while cleverly avoiding the spirit of a request. An example is a child who dumps things on the bed, dressers, or other places when he has been told to clean them off the floor; or the child who rakes the leaves from the lawn to the middle of the driveway and reports: "They're off the lawn."

Children use excuses that are not quite "irrational." It is difficult to challenge the credibility of a weak excuse. Expressions of hurt and pain on a child's face when his excuse is challenged wring the heart of the hardest adult. For example, a child who has been asked to vacuum the living room may say that he was not able to do it because the dog was very frightened that afternoon, and he needed to spend time with it. Another example is the child who usually creates a disturbance when taken to the market with Momma. After being told not to create a disturbance, he "accidentally" walks into a shelf and stubs his toe. The resulting hysteria is little different from his usual scenes.

Many children appeal to "hidden internal processes." They have an ache, feel sick, are afraid or "forget." A parent is not able to tell whether these complaints are true or not. This is exemplified by a child who is supposed to do the dishes after dinner, but says that he's not feeling well and needs to lie down. It's hard for a parent to deny such a request. But if the child is in his room playing actively an hour later (all pain and sickness having disappeared), it's also hard not to be angry.

Forgetting

That last point deserves to be expanded because one of the basic issues in teaching children to be responsible is the question "Who is responsible for remembering?" We doubt there is any parent or teacher who has not heard the statement "I forgot." Children may be competent and want to please parents, but if they have not taken responsibility for their own *memory*, they cannot be responsible.

Children remember what is important to them yet forget what is important to the parent or teacher. The same child who forgets *every day* to take the garbage out, remembers some vague promise made to him three weeks previously, often long after the adult has forgotten it.

Children's sense of time is different from adults. Very young children live in the present moment, rather than in the past or future. A child who is totally absorbed in some activity will tend to disregard a responsibility.

There are various devices that encourage children to remember, devices that can be relaxed as children grow and become better able to assume responsibility.

- **Write things out, and post them.** Keep copies of chore lists. Have a "message center." Parents can pin up children's duties in their rooms.

- **Don't remind children after they have assured you they have heard and understood.** Reminding children of things can become a bad habit; children then depend on it.

- **Establish as much regularity as you can.** Having things happen at regular, predictable times enhances children's ability to remember. Duties that are associated with regular events tend to be done better.

- **Don't be afraid to punish, if a child "forgets."** A mild punishment related to a chore that hasn't been done can act as a prod to the child's memory.

- **Remember what you said.** When parents forget, they give tacit permission for children to do so. Remember that one of the greatest sins a parent can commit, in a child's opinion, is to forget a promise. Do whatever you have to do to remember what you told a child—write it out, post a note, tie a string on your finger.

Children often believe that their agenda of activities is the most important in the family. When a child believes that, it is easy for him to disregard or "forget" his responsibilities. When children learn to remember their responsibilities, their relationships within and outside the home improve.

When parents respect the child's agenda from time to time, it helps to create the attitude in children that they too may have to forego current pleasures in order to satisfy the needs of others. But parents should not forego their own personal pleasures in order to accommodate the wishes of their children. As they grow, it is important for children to recognize that their personal agenda may have to take a back seat.

How Children Shift Blame

In order to avoid responsibilities, children use the strategy of shifting blame onto parents and teachers. Children who blame others for causing them to be unable to complete tasks, create the impression that unreasonable requests were made. By blaming, children indicate how powerless they are to fulfill their responsibilities.

By being powerless, a child can avoid responsibility. Power is expressed through decisions and choices. As long as others are responsible for decisions and choices, children remain blameless.

When adults accept responsibility for remembering what the child is to do, the child is no longer responsible for remembering. If a task is not completed, the child can say, "Well, you didn't remind me," or "You didn't tell me." If the adult believes that he is responsible for reminding the child, then the child is not responsible for doing the job, the parent is.

A child can shift blame by finding some way that the adult is responsible for a task not finished. For example, a child who has been asked to sweep off the porch but hasn't done it may say, "You didn't tell me where the broom was, and I couldn't find it." It is frustrating to challenge the child about it, because he will always come up with something like "I looked in the kitchen and the hallway." A parent finds it hard to believe the child didn't know the broom was kept in a certain closet for the past 4 years. The child can innocently say he never noticed.

Children can attack adults for not communicating clearly. Often adults *are* at fault in this since they do not always check whether communications have been received. The simplest technique is to ask the child to repeat the instructions, and to indicate whether there's anything that he does not understand. Children have some advantage when adults are unclear, because they have a "reason" for not completing the task. In the above example, the child can say: "You didn't tell me that the broom was in the closet." Since that statement is true, the parent is left feeling vaguely frustrated and manipulated.

Children shift blame by criticizing adults' character. By attacking the parent or teacher's sense of fairness, honesty or responsibility, children challenge the adult's integrity. For example, a child may accuse the adult of requiring more from him than from others in the family or classroom. Or the child may accuse the adult of not telling him in advance about something he would have to do. The accusation may be true in a given circumstance but adults must have authority to request things from children from time to time without prior warning, especially in unexpected circumstances. When personal characteristics such as fairness or honesty are attacked, adults often feel guilty, resentful or frustrated, which makes their relationships with children more difficult.

Children avoid responsibility by pointing out their parents' weaknesses. This is particularly true in the home. For example, a child who is requested to clean his room may argue that the parents' room is not a model of sparkling cleanliness. It is not possible or necessary for parents to do perfectly what they ask children to do. Since any weakness the child may point out will usually have some element of truth to it, a parent will pause and reevaluate his request. Such accusations then stimulate discussion and argument. And when parents and children argue, the job is not getting done.

Children are very good at finding parents' weaknesses. Children believe they can be irresponsible if they are convinced that parents are also irresponsible. In other words, an "After you, Alphonse" situation results in which the child implies that he will be better when you get better, but not before. In spite of all the time and energy parents put into managing and nurturing their families, children who seek to avoid responsibility will find some weaknesses in the parents' self-concept.

VIII.
How Children Hurt Others' Feelings and What to Do About It

Children are very powerful people. In a society that has become increasingly *child-centered*, children's impact on parents and teachers is often overlooked. It's easy to recognize that adults can hurt their children's feelings. It is also true that children can hurt adults. When parents and teachers deny their feelings are hurt by their children, it leads to hidden resentments and frustrations.

- The greatest weapon that children have is their ability to make adults feel guilty. This has been discussed at length in previous sections.

- Children are experts at hurting their parents' feelings by denying them individuality and uniqueness. When children accuse parents of being "just like a parent," or "like all up-tight adults," they deny that parents are special. Denying or disregarding someone's special qualities is a way of diminishing that person's self-esteem. All parents want to be important to their children, and children can hurt them by suggesting that they "don't care."

- When children accuse parents and teachers of inflicting pain or discomfort on them, parents' feelings are hurt because of the vague implication that the adult takes pleasure in the child's discomfort. None of us likes to be accused of being malicious. Such accusations often result in hurt feelings.

- When children don't live up to expectations, even minimal ones, parents' and teachers' feelings are hurt. Adults like to believe that a child's behavior is partly a result of their efforts. When children perform poorly, those adults feel they have done a poor job. Those who tolerate poor performance in children set up a situation for pain and frustration.

- When children trigger an adult's anger, that adult feels bad. Anger is the precursor of rage. If anger has been stimulated enough, the adult may sense that his rage is boiling beneath the surface. The possibility of expressing that rage increases. Adults who have allowed the relationship with their children or students to deteriorate to this level often have hurt feelings, and are prone to depression.

- Parents and teachers seek approval from children. When children withhold approval, in spite of all efforts, hurt feelings result. It is unlikely that children will give "gold stars" for good performance, but they do have many ways they *can* show approval, if they wish. When children don't, adults can be disappointed.

- When children don't live up to the ethical and behavioral standards set for them, feelings are hurt. If a child lies, cheats, or steals and is abusive or insensitive to others, adults are particularly hurt, because of the personal responsibility and personal failure they feel.

Since there are so many ways children hurt adults' feelings, there is no one technique to deal with them.

- Parents and teachers who feel *self-confident* and *in control* of their families and students and have their *authority affirmed* and responded to by their children and students, are much less likely to have hurt feelings.

- When communication is clear and consistent, and children understand adults' expectations and standards, they are less likely to hurt adults' feelings, or attempt to do so.

- Adults who deal with children's misbehavior in straightforward and reasonable ways can avoid being hurt. When parents and teachers are confident that they have methods for dealing with problems, and have clear goals set, their self-assurance protects them against hurt feelings.

- Adults who can discuss feelings with children, their own as well as the child's, can say when they're hurt, and work to resolve it. Children may not know they have hurt others' feelings, unless they are told in a way they understand.

Some adults believe that if children hurt their feelings, they have the right to hurt their children's feelings. "An eye for an eye and a tooth for a tooth." This kind of response supports a climate where people have "permission" to hurt each other's feelings. When adults try to avoid hurting children's feelings, and treat them with respect and dignity, children will not *want* to hurt their feelings.

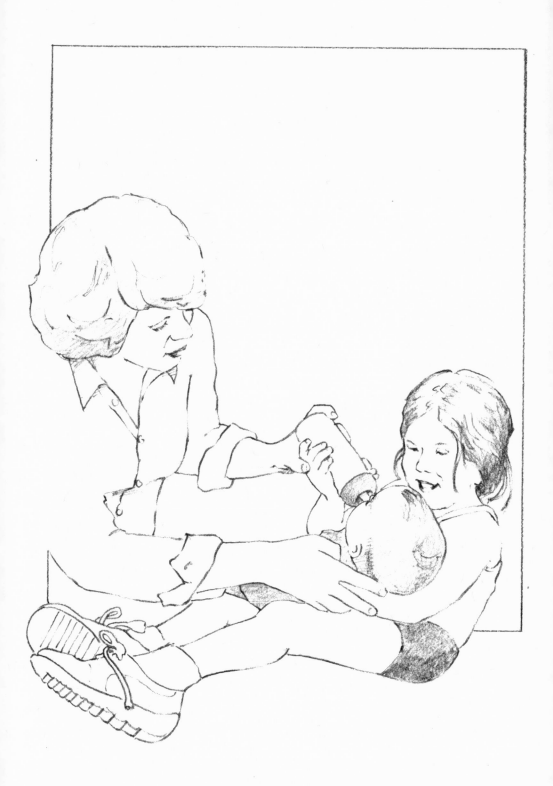

IX.
Parents as Models of Responsibility

Every family is unique. Such uniqueness needs to be respected. Each person brings to a new family his or her own early family experience. When people who have different backgrounds marry, a totally new situation for a new generation of children is created. Each family must respect the values, beliefs, and attitudes of each member. A family needs to function in a way that enhances the ability of each individual in it to gain maximum satisfaction from participation in family affairs.

The fact that one family is different from another does not mean that one family is better than another, or worse. Parents must determine for themselves what are reasonable expectations and what attitudes they want to emphasize within their own families. In some families work and productivity are emphasized as the most important values; in others, the quality of human relationships receives greater emphasis. This handbook can help all families use procedures which most effectively carry out their purposes.

Pick and choose among the suggestions offered in this handbook, and decide for yourself which most exemplify your own goals for being a parent. *The ultimate criteria of your success will be the satisfaction and comfort which all members of the family experience in your home.*

Parents who are irresponsible cannot teach their children to be responsible. Parents who blame others for their difficulties, who are indecisive, who forget, who manipulate others, who get others to make decisions for them, are models of irresponsibility. There is no formula for teaching children to be responsible that allows parents to act irresponsibly while their children become more responsible.

Children spend a lot of time observing parents' behavior and modeling it. When parents approach their tasks with a reasonable amount of good will, commitment, and decisiveness, children will tend to adopt these characteristics. It is especially important for parents to be models of responsibility when they deal directly with children. In these interactions, children learn much about responsibility.

Children learn to be responsible by seeing their parents do things that are difficult or hard to do. This does not only mean performing hard work. It also means controlling one's feelings, making decisions that are appropriate, considering the needs of others, and making hard decisions about children.

When parents are inconsistent, it is the child who knows it first. Parents' inconsistency is often the result of forgetting what they told a child. The one person who always knows when parents are inconsistent is the child. Children whose parents are inconsistent will come to believe that such inconsistency is OK in human relations. Excessive inconsistency is a form of irresponsibility.

Inconsistency should not be confused with flexibility. Being flexible means that a parent is willing and able to employ a variety of methods for reaching a consistent goal. If one way doesn't work, try something else. Being inconsistent means that a parent changes the goals, often unconsciously. Parents might decide that trying to hold a child accountable for some rule infraction is becoming too difficult. Rather than finding an alternative method for holding firm, they may change the goal, to preserve their own peace of mind, or "do it themselves."

Children learn from observing the way that parents deal with each other. When parents take responsibility for each other and the family in a forthright, honest and direct way, it is much easier for their children to take responsibility. Children who observe parents resolving conflicts in an amicable way will model that behavior also.

Once children have been given responsibility, parents should not confuse them, and encourage irresponsibility by taking it back.

Parents take responsibility back from children by:

- Remembering, when the child "forgets."

- Doing it themselves "because it's easier."

- Underestimating children's capabilities.

- Accepting children's labels of themselves as incompetent or irresponsible.

- Doing things for children so they will like parents, or stop hurting their feelings.

- Believing that only parents who work hard and do lots for their children are responsible, "good" parents.

It is difficult to stand back and watch a child struggle in order to learn how to do something. "Inner toughness" is required by parents who want to teach children to be responsible in a satisfactory way. Parents have to allow children to make mistakes and learn from them. Once parents are sure they have clarified their requirements, given children the alternatives they need, and taught them ways to fulfill duties, then it is important to stand back and allow children to experience the realities of becoming responsible human beings.

We do not intend to make parents feel guilty if they don't live up to these high standards. Nevertheless, to the extent that children see parents being responsible comfortably, their own ability to be responsible will be enhanced.

If parents are fair, clear about expectations, consistent in applying consequences, reward children for good behavior and follow through on promises made, children will come to believe that being responsible is a virtue.

X.
How Much Can Reasonably Be Expected of Children

This question is repeatedly asked by concerned parents who are interested in developing a system of responsibility and accountability in the home. Where people live, their level of income, the number of children in a family and many other variables distinguish one family from another, and make a simple answer to the question impossible.

The following guidelines may assist parents in reaching a decision in this matter:

- **All children need to be responsible for something in the home.** Parents need to arrange things so as to distribute the tasks of family maintenance and management among family members, and to give children some duties that will help them develop a sense of responsibility.

- **All children need to have an adequate balance between work and play;** they need time for being responsible to parents, and time for being responsible for themselves and their own activities. This balance will change as the child grows and develops.

- **How complex tasks are, and what standards for performance are expected of the child will change over time.** There will be some periods during the child's development when personal needs take precedence over some duties at home. When children join Scouts, or have other important activities outside the home, in-home responsibilities may need to be adjusted. Children need to have opportunities to learn about human relationships and other skills outside the home. But a child who develops extensive interests outside the home cannot be totally exempted from duties within the home. A balance between responsibilities outside and inside the home is very healthy for children.

- **Parents need to adjust expectations about how much a child is expected to do within the home,** so that a reasonable amount of time is required. Two or three simple tasks a day, if done well, do not require more than 10 to 20 minutes of a child's time. This is not unreasonable to expect of any child. Complex tasks that require a greater amount of time may occur periodically. If the child is forewarned, those tasks can be balanced with other demands on the child's time.

- **Organization of time, both within and outside the home, will increase the child's capability to perform tasks well.** When duties and times when things need to be done are clear, a child can take responsibility to organize his own time so that there is little conflict between duties at home and his own activities.

Many parents ask, "How old should a child be before he or she can begin receiving training in being responsible?" The answer to this is *as early as possible.* Initial learning about responsibility is encouraged through children's play. Parents can create "games" for the child to play that begin to establish attitudes and habits about expectations.

As soon as a toddler begins to move about, manipulate objects and understand simple language, he can be encouraged to put toys away, treat pets properly, take care of his room in simple ways, and be helpful to both parents in the tasks they perform. Toddlers love to express their skills by doing things that receive praise from parents, and that mimic adult behavior.

Even though a toddler of 2 or 3 may not have the capability to take out the garbage, it is possible to put a small amount of garbage in a paper bag and ask him to help a parent or older sibling. Likewise, when Mom or Dad is vacuuming, the little one can go along for the ride, becoming involved with and observing parents at work.

Parents need to recognize that the toddler's competence, sense of goals and ability to follow through on tasks, are limited. The child who "helps with the dishes" may do more splashing and getting wet than actually cleaning dishes, but he may pick up some clues about dishwashing. As long as an activity is fun and satisfying for children, they will continue to do it. Toddlers' interests are diverted quite easily, and their attention to one thing does not last long. Parents should take this into consideration, and not have unrealistic expectations.

Toddlers develop a "nay-saying" attitude. Even though they have been "helping" with a chore for some time, they may take a notion to say "no."

58

With a little coaxing, they may become involved again, or parents may offer an alternative activity to them.

As time goes on, these "playful" activities can become more and more regular. Toys always need to be picked up; garbage always needs to be taken out; dishes always need to be done; and the house always needs to be cleaned. Opportunities are always available for very young children to become involved in these duties on a regular basis. As a child repeats these activities and sees parents or older siblings doing them regularly, he will soon understand that such activities are a regular part of life in his family. A young child's interest in and commitment to such activities will wax and wane. The important thing is to have a climate in which a child is encouraged to believe there are *necessary* activities for him to perform.

Other examples of things that can be done very early in a child's life to promote a sense of responsibility are: have him put away books after they've been read; organize his room so that many of his toys or belongings have a special place; and teach him where to put things. He can help in the garden by digging holes and carrying dirt; he can help wash the car, especially on warm days in shorts or diapers, if parents anticipate that more water play than cleaning will occur.

These "play activities" are enhanced by parents making a game of them, and they are a critical part of a child's development. If parents create opportunities for children to help with tasks and duties early in toddlerhood, it is more likely that in the long run the child will maintain attitudes of responsibility.

XI.
How to Teach Children Responsibility

Developing a Child's Sense of Power

A child needs to develop a sense of power in order to have high self-esteem. *Having a sense of power means that a child has the resources, opportunities and capability to influence the circumstance of his own life.*

A child must have the opportunity to make choices and decisions, to exercise his competence, and to perform tasks consistent with his abilities. Opportunities for children to express the skills and competences that they *have* must be created. As their level of competence rises, new opportunities need to be available, so that children can practice what they know. Such competencies include both mental skills and physical ones—helping with chores around the house, for example, allows children to exercise the physical capabilities they have. As they grow, children become capable of performing more complex operations, and of improving their performance. They need continually expanding opportunities to demonstrate and use their skills.

In order for children to do anything, they need the resources that are requisite to the task. A child will have great difficulty keeping a room tidy, for example, if there are not adequate storage spaces. Most resources can only be provided by parents, since children cannot provide them for themselves.

Parents need to provide children with the resources required in order to develop the skills, knowledge and values they need as growing persons.

61

Games, books, toys, paper to draw on, stuffed animals, and many other things are important for children to have. Having such things allows children to learn how to care for things they value, and as a result, begin to care for the things that others value.

In order for children to fulfill responsibilities parents give them, they have to be capable of doing so. This means they have to have the physical skills, they have to understand why things need to be done, and have to understand the consequences for poor performance. Ensuring that they have a clear understanding of what parents want, and why, increases children's ability to perform at a higher level of competence.

These three factors (resources, opportunity and capability) are required so that children can develop a sense of personal power. That means being able to make decisions about their activities.

Teaching children to be responsible enhances their sense of power. Children who can act responsibly are more confident, know how to handle themselves and know how to gain rewards and praise. As a consequence they improve their own self-esteem.

Help Children Make Decisions

Making decisions and carrying them out is the way that children express their sense of power. *Children who have learned to be responsible make better decisions than those who haven't.* Parents and teachers can increase children's ability to make decisions by following these principles:

- Help children clarify the problem that is creating the need for a decision.

- Help children search for alternative solutions.

- Help children select one of the alternatives by evaluating the consequences.

- Help children evaluate the effectiveness of their decisions through feedback and discussion.

While it may not be possible to apply these four steps each time a child makes a decision, time and circumstances being limiting, it is good to keep them in mind, and use them when appropriate.

WHAT'S THE PROBLEM?

Children cannot solve a problem unless they know what the problem is. Tendencies to blame others and avoid responsibility, and limitations of age and experience, often confuse children about what the problem actually is.

62

When helping children clarify a problem, parents and teachers need to focus children's attention on what it is they *see and hear*, what it is they *feel* about the situation, and what they want to *change*.

Helping children clarify a problem does not mean telling them what the adult believes the problem is. It means rather that children are helped, through questions, to define the problem for themselves. Too much helpful advice can make children dependent on that advice or, alternatively, make children feel that they're not being heard. Children who feel they're not being heard soon stop coming for help.

When children learn to label their feelings accurately, their ability to make decisions improves. This is especially important in helping children to identify the problem. In discussing problems, adults need to provide the language and vocabulary, so that children can accurately identify what it is they feel. This means that children need to learn to describe their feelings, not only express them. Describing feelings gives a child perspective on himself, and more power over controlling his own feelings. The ability to control feelings is increased by understanding them. Sometimes a good decision can be made only if a child can control his feelings long enough to make it.

SEARCH FOR ALTERNATIVES

Here's where adults can offer advice. Children may not be able to generate alternative solutions, especially if the problem is charged with emotion. They will wish to find the one "best" solution.

Children's decision making ability is enhanced only if they have two or more alternatives from which to choose. It is best to withhold criticizing children's ideas, until there are several alternatives proposed. Adults should not be too critical of their own ideas until the child has a chance to hear them. Some alternatives they suggest may be frivolous or unrealistic, but may still be helpful in encouraging children to see that they are making a decision. Not even adults can come up with alternatives all the time, and in some situations the best solution is obvious.

Children may become impatient during the search for alternatives and want to rush into an impulsive decision. When adults offer alternatives, they slow the process down. Children become more aware of the decision making strategy, and gain perspective on themselves as well as the problem.

WHAT'S THE BEST SOLUTION?

Picking the "best" solution is the goal of decision making/problem solving. The best solution is one that solves the problem *and* makes a child feel good about himself. Such a solution has the least negative consequences and the most positive ones. Evaluating the consequences of various alternatives is the method for picking the best solution.

Sometimes the only way a child will find out the consequences of a decision is to make it and see what happens. Parents and teachers need to help children evaluate the risks, and be supportive and/or approving, depending on the results.

Older children often need to "test" adults' forecasts in order to find out whether they are correct. Even though they make decisions that can be foreseen as problematic, it may be necessary to not intervene, so that children do "learn from their own experience." Adults don't enhance children's decision making abilities by requiring that every decision be a "good" one, but rather by ensuring that they are aware of the fact they have made a decision. Suffering negative consequences can motivate children to be more rigorous in evaluating the consequences of future decisions.

HOW DID IT WORK OUT?

Evaluating the results of a decision helps children become more aware of the process. If a decision works out well, approval reinforces and punctuates the child's success. When a decision does not result in positive outcomes, it helps to review the alternatives again and analyze what went wrong.

The basic question is, "What went wrong?" not "What did you do wrong?" Evaluation means looking at the whole situation, not only the child's part in it. It is useful to have the child review the tactics he will use the next time the problem arises. You can help a child prepare for this by getting a clear picture in his mind of desirable alternatives, rather than emphasizing what he did wrong.

Children can be helped to learn about decisions when they can understand language and respond to it. "What toy do you want to play with?" "Which do you like better?" Giving children simple problems to solve ("What do you want to eat first, the pear or the meat?"), provides the opportunity to have control over something. Offering children increased opportunities to solve problems and make decisions *does not mean that adults turn over all major decisions to a child.* In learning how to teach children to make decisions, they will make mistakes. They may have to reclaim decision making authority, when they find that a child is "over his head." There is no absolute guideline; all children learn by trial and error, and they need to be protected from excessive harm resulting from the decisions they make.

Setting Rules and Limits

Children who grow up in a home that doesn't have clear rules and limits for behavior will experience great anxiety and confusion. If children are anxious and confused, it is difficult for them to exercise the self-discipline required to manage their own behavior. They are more likely to misbehave, and will have problems following directions and fulfilling responsibilities.

"Spoiled children" are not born that way. Children become spoiled as a function of their experiences. The absence of certain experiences is instrumental in spoiling children.

Common wisdom implies that children who are spoiled are given too much. In fact, the contrary is true. Children who become spoiled are not given enough of some things. They are not provided with enough clarity about what parents expect, have too few important responsibilities to fulfill, and are not held accountable, consistently, for what they do. No child can have too many toys. Since most children are selective about what they play with, a child who is given large numbers of toys only plays with a few of them anyhow, those that have become his favorites. But children who are not held to limits about what they can say or do, and are not taught to recognize others' needs within the family, will use their resources in ways that interfere with others, producing frustration, resentment and anger, in themselves and other members of the family. And later they will carry their attitudes with them into the classroom.

The parents of spoiled children tend to have hidden resentments and anger toward them. No parent actually "likes" a child who is excessively demanding and manipulative, or who has fits of hysteria or crying. This can only be headed off if parents have established rules in an adequate manner, clarified what's expected, established appropriate consequences, and followed through consistently.

Use Chores and Duties to Build Responsibility

The duties and chores required to maintain a home in an adequate way are also the basic ingredients that help children learn to be responsible. These are the building blocks for teaching responsibility.

Neither parents nor children want to be excessively burdened with the duties of family management. For this reason, it is fair and reasonable that such responsibilities be shared among the members of the family. As children observe parents going about duties in the household, and are inducted into doing them, they will gradually understand that such behavior is required, and that people within the family depend on each other.

Chores and duties are concrete; how, when, and by whom they should be done can be specified. Through learning these processes, children increase their skills and develop mental models of the way things are done. This will help them develop the ability to organize and manage their own resources.

Children who are not required to do "chores" early will lack skills in organizing themselves, setting goals, and working through complex tasks in their middle childhood and adolescence. Learning how to work, step-by-step through a chore helps children apply the same principles in their own work and play.

Learning to keep things organized results from having experienced things being organized. When a child participates physically, mentally and emotionally, in the organization of things within the home, his capability to do so in school and in other activities will be immeasurably increased.

Dealing with "external tasks" helps children to organize their "internal processes." Even growth in logical thinking is aided by learning the "logic" of ordinary household procedures such as putting toys away or cleaning one's room. Furthermore, being required to do chores helps children learn to deal with frustration and ambiguity. Children who do chores regularly become better problem solvers.

Be Consistent

Being consistent is the best way to let children know that adults mean what they say. Consistent application of a rule with mild punishment for breaking it will have more effect on a child in the long run than inconsistency and severe punishment. Consistency is a way for parents to show children they are aware of behavior. When he knows that adults are aware of his behavior, a child has added incentive to act appropriately.

By being consistent, parents and teachers help children feel secure. When they are inconsistent, children become anxious because they cannot predict what will happen. It sometimes seems that children misbehave in order to get adults to set limits.

Attempting to consistently apply a bad rule will result in resentment and anger in both the child and the adult. Inconsistent application of a good rule will result in the child's behavior not being controlled by the adult. Consistent application of good rules will promote order and discipline, allow for security, and promote good will. Most adults are less consistent than they should be, but think they're more consistent than they are.

Of course, when there is no clear and obvious set of rules, there is really nothing to be consistent about.

When parents and teachers mean what they say, it implies that they will take responsibility for following through on what they mean. When they behave in this way they act as models to children, and help them develop a sense of responsibility. Children more often than not listen to what parents and teachers say, and then evaluate subsequent actions, in order to find out whether they meant what they said and what they are likely to do about it. When children observe inconsistency, they learn that it is permissible to say one thing and do another. This is a basis for irresponsibility. When an adult makes a commitment to do something, or threatens to take a certain course of action, and then does not follow through, he has communicated clearly to a child that it is not necessary to follow through on commitments made.

Avoid Being Arbitrary

Arbitrary action means one of two things: the parent or teacher does something other than what he said he would do, or he does something the child was not warned about, and did not expect.

When a parent is arbitrary, it is hard for a child to predict what will happen as a result of what he does, especially how parents will react. An unexpected act increases the child's anxiety, fear and frustration, and he will resist performing tasks in a competent and adequate manner.

In order to avoid being arbitrary, parents and teachers need to: clarify what it is they want; communicate those expectations simply and directly to the child; and specify the consequences that will occur if the child acts consistently or inconsistently with those expectations. Without such clarification, arbitrary action is inevitable. Foresight about those things that might occur in a given situation will help parents and teachers act consistently and predictably. Acting arbitrarily will make children tentative and cautious in what they do. When given tasks to do, children will perform them incompletely or poorly, since they cannot predict accurately if the adult will intervene, or how the adult is going to react when the children believe the task is done.

In order to reduce arbitrary action, agreement between both parents about expectations and how to approach problems is important. If one parent says or does one thing and the other parent another, the child is automatically involved in a situation where someone is likely to be arbitrary. Even though each parent believes he or she is acting consistently, the child experiences arbitrariness and inconsistency.

Often parents and teachers don't give themselves enough time to make decisions reasonably. While doing something that is absorbing their whole attention, the adults may have to make a decision about something a child wants. At moments like this, many parents act arbitrarily, because they are distracted or because they are angry or frustrated. Parents would be better served if they were to say: "You'll have to come back in ten minutes and talk with me about that, because I cannot deal with it now." If a parent can prepare for it, he can more reasonably discuss the issue with the child, and come to a realistic resolution. Children often deliberately confront adults when they are busy since, by distracting, they may be able to get what they want.

Children need to be trained not to interfere when adults are busy. If adults consistently point out the need for self-restraint in such situations and follow through on promises to discuss the issue, children will learn that not interfering with parents and teachers when they are involved can work to their advantage.

Another characteristic problem situation for many parents is being interrupted by children when they're on the telephone. Many parents have solved this problem by setting a rule about not interfering, clarifying a punishment that will be applied if the child does so, and specifying when and how the child's problem will be dealt with (after finishing the phone call, parent and child will sit down and discuss it). If this is discussed as a general rule, and parents follow through consistently, it usually ends the problem.

There is one last issue to be considered.

Parents will be arbitrary sometimes, no matter how hard they try not to be. There are times when something must be done immediately, with no time for discussion. There are times when factors that are influencing parents' actions cannot be explained to children. There are times when parents are so upset, tired, or angry that being arbitrary is the only way to preserve mental health. Many parents find it hard to apologize to children, even though a simple apology may be all that's needed to improve relations. Explaining why a decision was made in a certain way, after the fact, may help children to understand parents' behavior. In other words, all parents act arbitrarily at times, and that's all right—as long as it's not the usual way they deal with their children.

Give Rewards for Being Responsible

Seeking rewards for good behavior is one of the motives that encourages children to behave appropriately. The other is the desire to avoid punishment. Children who are always punished for being irresponsible and rarely rewarded for being responsible, will develop an "unbalanced" attitude towards tasks and duties. They will seek to avoid punishment by manipulation, denial, lying or incompetence, and will find little virtue in being responsible. Parents and teachers who are serious about teaching children to be responsible should know how to apply rewards for positive behavior.

Children are very concrete. They are more likely to do things that they don't like to do if something special happens for them as a result of doing a task. Many parents worry when children go through "materialistic" stages. They may want to be "paid" for doing things, or try to negotiate some advantage for themselves for doing jobs in the home. Many parents fear that these attitudes imply a child is developing a bad character that will result in poor attitudes about responsibilities. Actually, it is quite normal for children to pass through this stage and points out the degree to which children seek concrete responses in order to evaluate the success or failure of their own actions.

By the time people become adults, many of their actions are motivated by internal rewards that they give themselves, i.e., feeling good about having done a job well. Adults have resources to use in order to give themselves rewards when they feel good, or have done something well, such as dinner in a restaurant after a hard day's work. Children lack control over financial resources they could use to reward themselves for positive behavior. It is important to provide some system of rewards that allows children to measure their own growth and success.

Working for rewards is a way children develop a goal-orientation. Having appropriate goals and working toward them is one of the characteristics of maturity. Children don't usually have adult-like goals they are working toward. As they recognize that they can get things they want through their own efforts, they become aware that having goals and working toward them is an advantage.

Working for rewards helps children become aware that they can establish their own goals for their own behavior, and ultimately reward themselves for reaching those goals. Concrete rewards help children establish concrete goals. They have a profound effect on growth and the ability to take responsibility.

Parents need to be aware of the variety of rewards they have available for children. In addition to financial or material rewards, things like time, attention, caring, sympathy, and good will, are all rewards that benefit children. There are times in the child's life when material rewards seem to be most important. As children learn that material rewards can be gained by them as a result of their performance, their self-confidence increases, and their sense of responsibility grows. This allows them to develop alternative reward systems.

XII.
Problems
with School

Children start school with many complex attitudes and capabilities. How successful they will be in school is largely determined by the way they handle limits and rules, and how they take responsibility. Children who have not been taught to be responsible at home, to perform chores and duties in a reasonable manner, and to understand parents' directives, will have a difficult time in school.

In a classroom that has 20 to 30 children, the need for rules, limits, order and accountability is great, even at the kindergarten level. If a child has not had experience in dealing with these issues at home, teachers have difficulty getting the child to adapt appropriately to a classroom situation. Most of the tasks children do in school are ones they have to take personal responsibility for.

In the modern school, much teaching is done through groups, but learning is still an individual process. Whether or not a student approaches school in a responsible manner, with a commitment to fulfilling his "part of the bargain," will determine whether or not school is a rewarding experience.

If children are prepared for school by having appropriate attitudes toward work, rules, and human relationships, they will receive lots of positive reinforcement from teachers. This will increase the likelihood of their success. If they have not been taught to be responsible at home, they are likely to act accordingly in school, and thus receive criticism and experience failure. Parents have a major role in this regard, i.e. in influencing their children's success in school.

Having a sense of responsibility and being able to perform adequately in school are closely related. In order to learn, children have to take significant amounts of personal responsibility. As they move up through the grades, learning processes become more complex and being responsible becomes more and more important.

Children who have difficulty in school blame peers, the learning situation, the teacher, the difficulty of the material, or other circumstances for interfering with their ability to perform adequately. This is a sign that a child has not yet taken responsibility for his own learning.

One of the things that children complain about in school is being bored. Boredom is often a sign that a child is not making choices among the available alternatives. It is true that some teachers do not teach in as exciting a way as others and that some do not provide challenging opportunities. But it is *also* true that in *every* classroom children have many opportunities to make decisions about what they will do, how much, and in what manner.

Children are making choices constantly within the classroom. They are making choices to perform, or not to perform, the tasks given them. Children act irresponsibly in school when the choices they make are inappropriate to the goals and purposes of the classroom and school, and when such choices produce failure and excessive criticism. In the overwhelming majority of classrooms, children will be rewarded for significant effort, irrespective of the level of their performance. Children who have learned to take responsibility will consistently make efforts, and their chances of school success will be enhanced, irrespective of their intellectual capability.

Teachers can assist children to develop a sense of responsibility in school by following the principles illuminated in this handbook. Chief among these is the organization of classroom processes so that children can make choices that are consistent with their capabilities and involve their interests. Teachers can ensure that children are confronted with the consequences of the decisions they make, and are shown alternative ways to accomplish classroom goals that lead toward success for them.

Parents aid their children's learning processes by providing a context in the home for children to take responsibility. They can also help by reinforcing the things that teachers need from children to enhance the learning climate in classrooms.

Children need to:

- pay attention to direction
- cooperate in learning tasks
- complete assignments on time
- work with, rather than against, the teacher
- manage their time effectively
- organize themselves and their materials
- participate in classroom activities
- be willing to make efforts

When they don't do these things, they undermine their own ability to learn, and they interfere with others.

When parents become aware that a child is acting irresponsibly in school, it may be necessary to have consequences occur at home. In that way, the child is clearly aware that parents want him to act appropriately in school, and are willing to take action to ensure it.

Staying in close communication with teachers is an important method for parents to gain the information they need. Frequently parents must take the initiative. Knowing whether a child is doing well or poorly, whether his behavior is improving or deteriorating, and whether he is trying or not, allows parents to provide rewards as incentives—or sanctions for misbehavior.

When parents and teachers work at cross-purposes, the child suffers. When parents and teachers work together to change children's behavior, dramatic results can occur.

XIII.
How to Tell When Children Are Responsible

Children act responsibly when they behave in ways that are appropriate in their family and in school without having to be reminded each time.

Many children follow orders very well, but this is not the same as being responsible. Being responsible means that a child evaluates a situation in the light of *his* experience and his awareness of parental expectations, and independently makes a decision to act in an appropriate way. Parents and teachers who constantly give their children orders, and take pride in seeing them carry out the orders, are not necessarily teaching children to be responsible.

When children take responsibility, it is unnecessary for parents and teachers to tell them how to act in every situation. Children adopt a pattern of appropriate behavior, both as a result of adult requirements, and from evaluating their experiences and reaching realistic conclusions from them. When they do so, they can begin to act responsibly.

A child is responsible when he:

- Performs regular duties without being told every time.

- Has reasons that he can specify for doing what he does.

- Does not blame others excessively.

- Is capable of making choices among alternatives.

- Can play or work by himself without undue discomfort.

- Can make decisions that differ from those of others in his group (friends, gangs, family, etc.).

- Has various goals or interests that can absorb his attention.

- Honors and respects parents' limits without excessive arguing.

- Can focus attention on complex tasks (relative to age) for some time without excessive frustration.

- Follows through on what he says he'll do.

- Acknowledges mistakes without excessive rationalization.

* * * * *

Notes

[1]See: *How to Raise Children's Self-Esteem*, Bean and Clemes, Enrich, 1980.

[2]For a more complete explanation of this process, see the companion work in this series: *How to Discipline Children Without Feeling Guilty*, Clemes and Bean, Enrich, 1980.

NOTES

NEW

TEACHER/PARENT RESOURCE BOOKS

• DISCIPLINE • RESPONSIBILITY • SELF-ESTEEM

These Resource Books offer practical techniques for dealing with children who have learning and/or behavioral problems. The books are written in an easy to understand, straight-forward style. They offer sound advice from family counselors in the areas that are most important to improving children's school performance.

Reynold Bean, Ed.M.   Harris Clemes, Ph.D.

HOW TO RAISE CHILDREN'S SELF-ESTEEM

This handbook shows how to help children improve: Self-confidence–Values and attitudes–Interaction with others.

HOW TO RAISE TEENAGERS' SELF-ESTEEM

Case examples illustrate: New approaches to teenager problems–Analyses of self-esteem problems–Guides to raising self-esteem.

HOW TO DISCIPLINE CHILDREN WITHOUT FEELING GUILTY

Adults can learn to direct children effectively by: Rewarding good behavior–Fitting chores to the child–Being consistent with discipline.

HOW TO TEACH CHILDREN RESPONSIBILITY

This handbook defines responsibility and provides practical activities for teaching responsibility: Helps children solve problems in school and at home.